HINDU PHILOSOPHY IN A NUTSHELL

HINDU PHILOSOPHY IN A NUTSHELL

EDWARD B. WARMAN

GYAN

Published by

GYAN

Gyan Publishing House
5, Ansari Road
Daryaganj, New Delhi-110002
Phone: 011-47034999, 9811692060
E-mail: books@gyanbooks.com

Distribution Network
gyanbooks.com
India, USA, Canada, UK, Australia

ISBN: 978-93-6920-409-0 (PB)

First Published, 1910

2nd Impression 2025

Printed at: Gyan Press, Delhi.

HINDU PHILOSOPHY IN A NUTSHELL
Author: EDWARD B. WARMAN

HINDU PHILOSOPHY IN A NUTSHELL

Vigorously Yours,
Edward B. Warman.

HINDU PHILOSOPHY IN A NUTSHELL

BY

EDWARD B. WARMAN, A. M.
AUTHOR OF "THE PHILOSOPHY OF EXPRESSION," "THE VOICE—HOW TO TRAIN IT," "GET WELL; KEEP WELL," ETC., ETC.

CHICAGO
A. C. McCLURG & CO.
1910

PREFACE TO THE SERIES

THERE are two reasons why I have written these books: first, in response to thousands of my pupils throughout this country and Canada who desire the instruction in a more tangible form than simply through the medium of the voice; second, that the general public may have the result of thorough, honest, and unbiassed investigation extending throughout a period of thirty-five years

Having kept abreast of the times, I am fully aware of the conclusions other writers have reached, especially on spiritism; and am further conscious of the fact that, with few exceptions, I do not, in the main, agree with these. However, my decisions have in no way been influenced by any writer, not even by my friend, the late Dr. Thomson Jay Hudson, whom I first met in 1899. When our paths converged, we found we had been travelling on parallel lines for twenty-five years. Comparing notes, I was pleased to learn that we had arrived, practically, at the same conclusions; therefore, there may appear to be much of Hudson in my writings, and it could not well be otherwise, especially on spiritism. I felt highly honored to have so great an authority bear so corroborative testimony.

By consulting the topics treated it will be observed that I have covered a much wider field than those who have preceded me, having touched upon every phase of Psychic Phenomena. This I have done as briefly and concisely as possible and practicable, and while my decisions are positive, they are neither arrogant nor dogmatic.

E. B. W.

LOS ANGELES, CAL.
August 1, 1910.

THE following letter, which speaks for itself, is from the late Dr. Thomson Jay Hudson, the author of "The Law of Psychic Phenomena," etc.:

No. 10 Ninth St., S. E.,
Washington, D. C., May 2, 1900.

I consider Mr. Edward B. Warman the peer of any man in his line; in fact, I know of no one who covers so wide a field. His experiences in Mental Telegraphy are equal to any I have ever known; he is the most practical psychologist it has ever been my pleasure to meet; his explanation of Hypnotism removes all fear; his sifting of the grains of truth from the Christian Science doctrine leaves nothing to be desired; his exegesis of Spiritism is scientific and logical, acknowledging, as every thorough investigator must, the alleged phenomena, but denying, as every logician must, the alleged cause. His Suggestions to Mothers are simply invaluable.

I heartily commend him for his sound doctrines.

Yours faithfully,
Thomson Jay Hudson.

Good words, good thoughts, good deeds be your unremitting efforts. —ZOROASTER.

Do not unto others as you would not they do unto you. —CONFUCIUS.

Love your enemies, bless them that curse you, do good to them that hate you, and pray for them which despitefully use you and persecute you. —CHRIST.

INTRODUCTORY

THERE are many persons in this country wasting time and money, as well as energy, each one thinking to become proficient in the Yoga teachings and thereby to develop into a full-fledged Yogi.

Such knowledge is extremely difficult of attainment, and its practice is impossible in this Western world. Not that I would belittle the general trend of the philosophic thought, for it is essentially uplifting; it appeals to what is best and noblest in man. From the Hinduistic point of view it aims to get at the soul and to put into its hands the reins of the mind and body. In its beautiful toleration it is well worthy of the strongest commendation. But its practices, in their completeness, are not for us; and anything short of that will never make a Yogi even in India, where everything is favorable for such a consummation.

The reading and the study of the philosophy, however, will give one the Hindu idealists' conception of God, of infinity, of man and his relations to the whole.

It is my purpose to record, as briefly and tersely as possible, with but few comments, the general points of interest and such information, in a condensed and comprehensive form, as will give the reader the main points of belief, not the practices, of this ancient philosophy.

It is to the teachings and writings of that genial soul, Baba Bharati, and the well beloved, the late Swami Vivekananda, that I am especially indebted for the mere outline given herein. For a more comprehensive view of this interesting subject I would recommend the perusal of "Krishna" by Baba Bharati, and "The Vedanta Philosophy" and kindred books by Vivekananda.

I have also been privileged to make some excerpts from the advance sheets of "Book on India" by my esteemed friend, Dr. Paul Edwards.

E. B. W.

HINDU PHILOSOPHY IN A NUTSHELL

What is this Philosophy? — The Hindu Triad — Explanatory — The Bhagavad Gita — Buddha — Om — Vedas — Guru —Krishna — The Garden of Eden — Eden — Adam — Eve — The Tree of Life —The Tree of Knowledge — The Aura — Karma — The Astral Body — Reincarnation — The Vedanta Philosophy — The Vedas — The Four Ages — The Golden Age — The Silver Age — The Copper Age —The Iron Age — The Deluge — The Caste System — The Caste Body — The Four Stages of Life — First Stage — Second Stage — Third Stage — Fourth Stage — The Five Paths of Yoga — Hatha Yoga — Karma Yoga — Raja Yoga —Gnana Yoga — Bhakti Yoga — Another View of Yoga Philosophy — Raja Yoga — Yama — Niyama — Asana — Samedhi — Pranayama — Poem by Hindu Sage — Comments on Hinduism — Persian Yogis — A Wonderful Discovery — The Buddhist's Religion.

THIS philosophy is a species of asceticism among the Hindus, which consists in " a complete abstraction from all worldly objects, by which the votary expects to obtain union with the universal spirit, and to acquire superhuman faculties."

When we of the Western world reach the point of complete abstraction from all worldly objects, we ourselves shall have been "completely abstracted" therefrom. Asceticism is not necessary; moderation and the control of the physical is our course in the Occident.

Some writer has well said: "The esoteric Hindu is too self-absorbed. His care for his own soul, in abstracting it from the mists and delusions of the sense-world, though highly creditable, has yet the tinge of selfishness; for he does not leave his light to shine for others, he even outcasts his own brethren. His Western brother of the same esoteric type is not unspiritual; he lives reverently, even if not so contemplative; and aside from a broader intellectual life, his spirituality has love for its basis, a love that is content with nothing less than the salvation of the whole world."

Paul, the philosophical expounder of the Gospels, who was undoubtedly as great an initiate of occult law as any of to-day, expresses himself most tersely in the familiar verses: "Though I speak with the tongues of men and of angels, and have not charity, I am become as sounding brass or a tinkling cymbal. And though I have the gift of prophecy, and understand all mysteries . . . . and have not charity, I am nothing."

Many that are seeking occult power desire it not for their soul's sake, but for their selfish aggrandizement. And when they obtain it with this selfish taint, they are far the worse for it. They are Fausts that would sell their souls for a pittance of power. This is far more the case in the Orient than in the Occident, for the active whirl of our busy world is not over-conducive to occult development.

In the East we find a hot atmosphere, a luxuriant vegetation, and stupendous mountains; and the form the religion takes is that of power, subtlety, contemplation, stillness, repose, rest, sleep, and entrancement. The religion culminates in the ascetic life with its diet of fruit, vegetables, and cereals, and its consequent soul power—entrancement and magic.

In the West, on the other hand, we

find a more temperate climate and a more active life, a larger brain and a manifestation of a wider range of the intellectual and practical life; and while we find the same prayer and contemplation and the same sacrifice of the bodily reserves as in the East, we find also less subtlety, less idealism, less repose and more energy, a severer standard of truth, and a more practical benevolence.

THE HINDU TRIAD

The triad of Hindu gods consists of:

1. Brahma. The One First Cause, the Creator of the Universe, the One Existence, the Absolute. The age of Brahma is the duration of creation,—311,040,000,000,000 human (lunar) years.
2. Vishnu. The Preserver, who takes care of the universe, and who becomes incarnate from time to time to help mankind.
3. Siva. The Destroyer, and the Conqueror of Darkness.

. . . .

EXPLANATORY

BHAGAVAD GITA. The Holy Song, a gem of Indian literature, containing the essence of the Vedanta Philosophy.

BUDDHA. The Enlightened, the name given to one of the greatest incarnations recognized by the Hindus; born sixth century B. C.

OM, *or* OMKARA. The most holy word of the Vedas. A symbolic word, meaning the Supreme Being, the Ocean of Knowledge, and Bliss Absolute.

VEDAS. The Hindu Scriptures, consisting of the Rig-Veda, the Yajur-Veda, the Sama-Veda, the Artharva-Veda; also the Brahmanas and the Upanishads, comprising the hymns, rituals, and philosophy of the Hindu religion.

GURU. A dispeller of darkness. A religious teacher who removes the ignorance of the pupil. A real guru is a transmitter of the spiritual impulse that quickens the spirit and awakens a genuine thirst for religion.

KRISHNA. The most popular of the Hindu divinities, usually held to be the eighth incarnation of the god Vishnu. He appeared in India about 1400 B. C. Most of his teachings are embodied in the Bhagavad Gita. He comes to this earth once in seventy-one Divine Cycles; that is, once in three hundred million or more human (lunar) years.

. . . . . .

THE GARDEN OF EDEN (Baba Bharati)

EDEN. A corruption of the Sanscrit word *Adhan,* signifying home, the Garden of Eden being the whole earth.

ADAM. A corruption of the Sanscrit word *Adhim,* which means primeval.

EVE. A corruption of the Sanscrit word *Heva,* which means life and love; Mother of Creation.

The Adams and the Eves were they of the Golden Age; Adam, the typical man; Eve, the typical woman. In that age, all men were as one, and all women were as one.

. . . . . .

THE TREE OF LIFE

Living on the Tree of Life, and eating of the Fruit thereof, was living in the essence of love, the inmost life and force of all existence.

. . . . . .

THE TREE OF KNOWLEDGE

Those who look outward and try to draw happiness from without, from *material* things, eat for the first time of the fruit of the Tree of Knowledge.

The Fall of humanity dates from the knowledge of material pleasures. The first hankering for it is the persuasive voice of the Evil One, called in Sanscrit, Māyā, which means *illusion;* that which is unsubstantial to the inner sight, yet seems and looks substantial to our outer (material) sight.

. . . . . .

THE AURA

The word *Aura* is from the Sanscrit word *Ar,* meaning the spoke of a wheel; *Ara,* full of spoke-like shoots of radiance from any centre.

The centre of our Aura is our mind. Aura, therefore, is the radiance of the mind, which permeates and envelops our body in an oval shape, and generally extends one cubit (eighteen to twenty-two inches) outside of our body.

The Aura, and reflections of thought-impressions on the Aura, are visible only to the spiritual and psychical sight. The illumined saints and yogis who have developed this sight see not only this Aura, but also the reflections of the thought-impressions, which they can read and interpret as we read and interpret words.

These reflections are called the characters of the mind—the hidden pictures (*chitra-gupta*) of human conduct—which reveal the past, the present, and the future history of a human soul to those who can decipher them.

From the Aura these characters are reflected again upon the ether, which receives the impression and keeps the record of each external and internal event in Nature. The ether is the storehouse of the records of all human and natural happenings and vibrations. It is from this storehouse of all mental records that true clairvoyance draws its inspired messages and revelations.

A fully developed Yogi can learn the detail of events which occurred ten thousand years ago, or of any time, and can tell of any present or future occurrence in any part of the world, by concentrating upon the ether, the all-knowing ether.

. . . . . .

KARMA

The word *Karma* is from the Sanscrit root *Kri,* which means *to act.* Karma is synonymous with our word Fate; it is the inevitable consequence of one's deeds; therefore one's acts are considered as fixing or determining one's lot in each succeeding incarnation.

Man is the conscious embodiment of the blended forces of his past actions; actions of previous conscious embodiments, born of the forces of still more previous embodiments.

Action proceeds from thought. Thought is the source and spring of action. No action is possible without its producing cause (thought), which is a phase of the mind's volition. All our thoughts are impressed on our mind the moment they form themselves, in condensed pictures. The more powerful a thought, the deeper the impression upon the mind. Weak, undeveloped thoughts make superficial impressions and are liable to wear off. The impression of a powerful thought is likewise rubbed off by the force of a strong counter-thought. An angry thought, for instance, prompts us to a bad action, but before it is reduced to action, our reason sometimes intervenes, argues against it, and convinces us of its error, which induces repentance. The stronger the counter-thought of repentance, the quicker and more effectively it rubs off the impression. But if the thought is reduced to action, the impression is deep and enduring, and requires the aid of absolutely sincere burning repentance to destroy that impression.

These thought-impressions on the mind are called seeds of Karma. A life of worldy joy and comfort is due to good Karma and self-denial in some previous existence. A life of sorrow and hardship is due to bad Karma.

Dr. Paul Edwards, speaking of Karma, says: "Hinduism teaches that we are pursued in the next world by the offences committed in this life; that whatever reward is due us will be found awaiting our arrival in the next life. It teaches a man may lead a bad life successfully even without being visited with pangs or punishment in this life; that he may live a life of villainy undisturbed by remorse or any adverse conditions. For this reason a careful account is kept in the next life of all his deserts in this, and a final adjustment is had when he departs for, or arrives in, the celestial abode. Present Hinduism teaches that the highest reincarnation is to become a Brahman."

. . . . . .

THE ASTRAL BODY (Baba Bharati)

It is the general belief of modern humanity that the human body is made up of flesh and blood alone. This is true as far as the physical body is concerned. But there is another body, within us, finer than the physical, which is the real body, and of which the physical body is the outer casement.

This real body is called the astral body. The whole human body is like a clock, of which the physical covering is its case, and the astral body its works. To know ourselves as nothing but our physical body, is the densest, narrowest, and most mischievous ignorance.

The materials of our physical body are supplied by our parents, but the astral body we supply ourselves. The astral body is our permanent body. It puts on new flesh garments from time to time. When it slips into a new flesh garment, that is called birth; when it slips out of it, that is called death. But, really, the astral body lives on forever and ever, and never ceases to exist, unless we find the means and take measures to destroy it.

. . . . . .

REINCARNATION

Reincarnation means rebirth; rebirth means being born again *in the flesh, after death.*

Into the vigor of the blood of a spiritual soul no wicked astral spirit can enter. Its pure aura repels such spirits and admits only kindred spirits seeking rebirth, drawn to it by Karma or affinity.

Much suffering is the lot of the ordinary soul while growing in the womb, on account of its cramped consciousness and the narrow space in which it is confined.

After the sixth month it has a wonderful experience. The veil shrouding its past existence is suddenly lifted, and the memories of all its past births rush across its mind.

It even witnesses the scenes of thousands of its previous existences, and also realizes the reason of the pain and sorrow suffered during all these existences—the reason of its having attached itself to material objects and having disregarded the development of its spiritual self; its having been unmindful of its duty to its Maker and its fellow-man. This realization crushes its mind with contrition, and it weeps and prays to God to forgive it, and promises to live a life of devotion to Him in the future.

This goes on for three months together until it is born, when, at the touch of the earthly atmosphere, all these memories vanish and are once more drowned in oblivion. It is from the pain of this shock that it cries out at the time of birth.

No conception can take place without a disembodied soul—a human germ—entering the human seed when planted in the human soil. The juice of the seed and the juice of the soil form but the physical body of the child; the astral body, which is encased in the physical body, comes from without to dwell in that state, and leaves the developed physical body at death, which is nothing but the total disorganization of the physical body. The astral body never dies.

. . . . . .

THE VEDANTA PHILOSOPHY
(Vivekananda)

Vedanta, from Veda, *wisdom,* and Anta, *the end.* Veda, the ancient sacred literature of the Hindus.

There are two schools of Vedanta, the old and the new. The old possesses the true interpretation of the

Aphorisms; the new is deluded by their false interpretations. The new is only about two thousand years old, and has a small number of adherents.

The old school holds that the universe is composed of the ever changeful manifestations of the will (energy) of the One Changeless Deity.

The new school calls the whole universe—in fact all that is visible and perceptible—Mayā (illusion) in the sense that it never existed, does not exist now, and never will exist. All that exists is Brahma, the Divine Essence, and we are That. All else is illusion wrought in our mind through ignorance.

Whence is this ignorance which has such power of illusion over our mind and senses? What is it? Whence does it come? The Neo-Vedantist answers, "It is something inexplicable."

His Māyā is inexplicable; it is the argument of one in darkness himself. This New Vedantic thought has done and is doing more harm to the world than any other religious theory. It is a worse delusion than the delusion of Māyā.

THE VEDAS*

"The right to read the Vedas incurs the most solemn obligation to keep their teachings from every living creature, especially from every lower caste. To divulge one word of the Vedas would mean to be hurled ignominiously from the high station and never to be again recognized. While they claim to possess the very truths necessary to save men's souls, yet they selfishly decline to divulge them to others, who may be ever so anxious for salvation. Instead of helping the distressed lower castes with ameliorating light and truth, the priests point them to the idol-gods, where they grovel in the vilest superstitions, fully believing that the great wisdom of their priests has shown them the true salvation in those images.

"To become a learned Brahman priest one has to commit the Vedas to memory, learn Sanscrit and the Mantras. He needs to know none of the sciences, none of the great laws of na-

*From Dr. Paul Edwards's "Book on India."

ture and of God. The Aryan Vedas are held to be of divine origin, the same as the Christian Bible, the Talmud, the Koran, and the fragmentary code of the Parsis.

"The persevering Faquir, or Sadhu, who practises his merciless austerities on his own body, is a far better man than the Brahman. I respect the poor saint who lies on spikes and nails, or the one whose hands are upheld from boyhood until Nature nails them there irrevocably, or the one who swings head downward over fire, as I believe him to be more conscientious than the inhuman priest who points his creeping, crawling devotees to the image-gods. I have watched these sincere devotees practise these awful austerities on their quivering tortured flesh, all for truth's sake as they believe it."

. . . . . .

THE FOUR AGES (Baba Bharati)

These are known as the Golden Age; the Silver Age; the Copper Age; the Iron Age.

It is in the last of these that we of

the twentieth century are now living; not very complimentary, but nevertheless true, as may be seen by the following classification:

The Divine Cycle is typical of the Fruit.

The Golden Age is typical of Ripeness.

The Silver Age is typical of Overripeness.

The Copper Age is typical of Rottenness.

The Iron Age is typical of Complete Rottenness.

THE GOLDEN AGE occurred nearly three million human (lunar) years ago. It covers a period of one million, seven hundred and twenty-eight thousand human years. Men of this period average thirty-one and one-half feet in height; can live one hundred thousand years and die at will.

Every age has a Junction period and a Degeneration period, called in the Hindu Scriptures the Twilight periods. The periods are of equal length. The Morning Twilight period of the Golden Age (Satya Yuga) is four hundred divine years, equal to one hundred and forty-four thousand human years. Of the same length is its Evening Twilight period.

The Evening Twilight period may be called the Degeneration of the Golden Age. It is then that Raja—activity—presents itself, and people begin to turn to material pleasures.

THE SILVER AGE covers a period of one million, eighty thousand human years. Men of this period average twenty-one feet in height. The average life in this age is ten thousand years.

There are no carnal relations in either the Golden or the Silver Age; but in the Silver Age men and women live together as husband and wife; yet in both ages the women give birth to children.

The child is conceived in the womb of the mother at the wish and command of the husband. The wife asks her husband for a child, and the husband of the Golden Age (who is a miniature creator in the potency of his mind-force) says, "So be it," and the wife at once conceives. But she has no pain of child-carrying or childbirth to suffer from. The child is born soon after, and, ofttimes, almost immediately.

In the Silver Age, the conception takes place in some cases in the same manner; and in some cases through the eating, by the wife, of *charoo,* a mixture of boiled rice, milk, sugar, and butter, magnetized by mystic words or the will-force of a psychic husband, or a saint, or a Brahman—a magnetism which draws into the preparation a disembodied spirt, who passes into the body of the wife through the food.

THE COPPER AGE covers a period of seven hundred and twenty thousand human years. Men in this period average ten and one-half feet in height. The trees become less in height, less fruitful, and the fruit less sweet than in the Silver Age. Cows give less milk, and crops are less abundant despite the best efforts of cultivation. Wild animals become more ferocious. Most animals can speak in the Silver Age; but now only some of them, the higher ones, are blessed with that power during the major portion of it.

People in the Copper Age become more and more outward-looking generally, especially the Sudras (the lowest of the four great castes), some of whom, having become filled with dense Tama (darkness), revolt against all laws and discipline, and turn into thieves and robbers. The Veda in the Copper Age has, for the first time, to be studied and its truths practised in two parts—the philosophical and the ceremonial.

It is not until this Copper Age that husbands and wives begin to have carnal relations. During the Golden Age and the greater part of the Silver Age all men and women are what Christians call virgin-born.

The fuss that is made (in this Western country) about the immaculate conception succeeds only in exciting a smile of pity in the Shastra-enlightened Hindu, a smile of pity for the ignorance of the facts in the past history of the human race, of which they seem to know so little and care less to know more. The fact that in the Golden and the Silver Ages, immaculate child-conception generally prevailed ought to open their eyes.

In the Copper Age, therefore, the decrease of spirituality takes away this power, and so the material of the physical body has to be supplied by the physical vigor of the father and the blood of the mother, to enable a disembodied spirit to enter the womb and grow into a child.

THE IRON AGE (the age in which we now live), covers a period of three hundred and sixty thousand human years. The average height of men in this age is five feet, nine inches. The average age of man should be one hundred years, but this is the exception rather than the rule, owing to the general violation of Nature's laws.

At the end of the Iron Age, the Fruit of the Divine Cycle having become fully rotten, is reduced to seed, out of which springs the sprout of the Golden Age.

The usual Iron Age, the last section of every Divine Cycle, is much more dense with Tama (darkness), than the one in which we are now living. This is due to the fact that Sri Krishna, himself the fullest incarnation of the Supreme Deity, came on earth to dwell among men for a period of one hundred years.

(This seems to have been a special dispensation, for, as a rule, this embodiment of Para-Brahm comes to dwell among men only once in seventy-one Divine Cycles—306,720,000 human years.)

According to the Hindu almanacs, about five thousand years only have passed since Krishna's departure.

By the coming of Krishna, not only the thirty-six thousand years forming the Junction period of Kali (the Iron Age) has been destroyed, but also almost half of the Kali proper (three hundred and sixty thousand years), has been likewise destroyed. He thus, in a measure, is supposed to have sanctified the soil of the earth-plane with the all-purifying touch of his Lotus Feet.

It is believed, however, that this present Kali (Iron Age), with its rapidly increasing accumulation of sin, may come to an end in less than ten thousand years, its conventional period of existence (three hundred and sixty thousand years) being condensed to that short space of time.

. . . . . .

During the Junction Period of the Golden Age, covering one hundred and forty-four thousand human years, the sprout coming from the seed of the Iron Age grows into a flowering tree, which bears fruit with the commencement of the Golden Age proper.

In the Golden Age, say the Hindu books, life is sustained by the *marrow* of the bones. Man lives as long as there is marrow in his bones.

In the Silver Age, life is centred in the strength of the *bones*. Man lives as long as his bones sustain their strength.

In the Copper Age, life is centred in the *blood*. Man lives as long as there is blood in the body.

In the Iron Age, life is sustained by *food* alone. With the decrease of spirituality in every succeeding age, the root of vitality has been transferred from marrow to bone, from bone to blood; but in this present age (the

Kali, or Iron) that root of vitality is destroyed.

. . . . . .

THE DELUGE

Yes, the Hindus had their Deluge; not only one but "many cataclysms, each one lasting seventy-one Divine Cycles (306,720,000 human years). Six of these have already passed. In each case the oceans surge up and cover the entire earth with their waters, even the highest peaks of the Himalayas."

They, too, had their Manoo (Noah) for each period. They claim that their word *Manoo* has been distorted into the word *Noah*. " This man was the most virtuous and spiritual of the time, almost as pure and spiritually powerful as Brahma, the Creator; a man whom the spirit of corruption failed to touch; a man possessed of uncommon physical beauty."

They, too, had their Ark which, in due time and in accordance with the foreknowledge given by Brahma, in the form and guise of a fish, was piloted to the highest peak of the Himalayas.

"It was on this peak, in a holy forest, that this man (King Satyavrata) was, for many hundred years, engaged in meditation and spiritual austerities."

In the course of time "the Ark appeared and into it went King Satyavrata (Manoo) and seven Rishis of the Great Bear (seven illumined beings, seers of thoughts; those possessed of super-sensuous knowledge), also all kinds of seeds of all trees, plants, shrubs, and creepers; also pairs of all animals and creeping things."

The Ark was tossed about on the huge waves seventy-one Divine Cycles (306,720,000 human years), but was preserved by the Divine Fish; and, eventually, when the waters had subsided and the highest peak of the Himalayas was visible, this Divine Fish drew it thence and said in a pleasant voice, "O ye illumined ones, bind the boat for a while to this mountain-peak." It is known to this day as the Boat-Binding Peak.

When the Ark was safely tied, the

Fish said again to the Rishis: "I am Brahm of Brahma, the Creator. I have taken the form of a Fish to save you all from the Flood. Now this Satyavrata will be known as Vaivaswata Manoo. He will, by the grace and power of his Yoga, create all mobile and immobile beings of the earth, gods and asuras and men." So saying the Fish vanished.

(This Manoo incarnates himself as a Rishi toward the end of every Golden Age. His term of office—306,720,000 human years—would make men of this day more ambitious than ever as office-seekers, but it should be remembered that he was *"a man whom the spirit of corruption failed to touch."* As we are now living in the twenty-eighth Cycle, his term of office has not half expired. Think of it! Only forty-three more Cycles to serve; only 185,760,000 human years! Drawing conclusions from the figures given in the Hindu books, many millions of years have gone by since the last flood, and many millions more will pass ere another. In the meantime, brethren, do not worry.)

. . . .

THE CASTE SYSTEM

The object of this is to preserve harmony, order, etc. While in the Golden Age there is but one family, in the Silver Age there are four families or castes. These are divided according to actions, habits, inclinations, etc.

The Brahmans are considered the head of the other castes, inasmuch as they still dwell in Brahm,—the Spirit of God.

. . . . . .

THE CASTE BODY

Head—The Brahmans, representing Wisdom.

Arms—The Kshatriyas, representing Strength.

Loins—The Vaishyas, representing Vigor.

Feet—The Sudras, representing Service.

The first are given to meditation on God and to the study of the Veda.

The second, to rule the two other castes with the aid of the Brahmans.

The third, to till the land and raise cattle only to serve God's creatures.

The fourth, to serve the three pure and spiritual upper castes for the purpose of absorbing their spiritual magnetism through association and examples.

All three of the castes, that is, second, third, and fourth, are expected to cultivate devotion to the Supreme Being by loving service rendered to His devotees.

A caste-birth is dependent upon Karma (actions). If one of low caste so wills it, he can become a high Brahman in the next incarnation, if he succeeds in developing his higher soul-consciousness.

. . . . . .

THE FOUR STAGES OF LIFE

First—Spiritual Pupilage.
Second—Householdership.
Third—Asceticism.
Fourth—Wandering Friarship.

First Stage. At the age of *twelve* the one who aspires to this spiritual development goes to reside with a Guru (spiritual guide) to study the Veda (spiritual, mental, and physical discipline).

The Guru feeds, clothes, and lodges

the pupil or pupils in his own abode free of any charge or consideration whatever.

If the student obtains this practical realization of the Essence of Existence, he remains for the rest of his life in this stage of spiritual pupilage. But he is no more a pupil; he becomes a teacher of pupils, a Guru.

SECOND STAGE. If, however, after staying twelve years, he fails to have this grasp of the soul of wisdom, he leaves the Guru, returns to the family, takes a spiritually inclined wife, and becomes a householder.

Still, his object is a realization of the Truth. This involves daily study of the Veda; simple and sparing meals; the means of living, honestly earned; hungry and needy beggars satisfied according to means and ability; parents, wife, family, poor relatives and dependents, and devoted servants must be supported, loved, and made happy.

All legitimate wishes and wants of the wife must be satisfied; she must be cherished with affection and respect, and regarded as the presiding deity of the household economy.

If during the household life the Truth is realized, the householder remains at home during the rest of his earthly days, and has no need to go into the third stage of life; for realization of the Truth is the end and aim of life in all its stages.

If this is not obtained after twenty-four years of family life, the householder must enter the third stage, the Ascetic.

THIRD STAGE. He must leave home with his wife, retire from worldly life and interests, live in a secluded forest place near home, practise austerities (physical and mental), and purge the mind of material inclinations; all of this for a period of twelve years.

If realization of Truth is obtained, he remains in that stage for the rest of his life, imparting the realized knowledge and wisdom to all who may come to him.

FOURTH STAGE. If he fails in this realization, he returns home with his wife. If he has a son to support the family, he leaves home and family, with the permission of his parents and wife, and enters the fourth stage, that of Holy Wanderer, to tread the path of Freedom and Truth all alone, surrender all ties of worldly life, and surrender himself—body, mind, and soul—to the search for Truth. He must keep his mind on the one thought; live on one simple, spare meal a day, enough to satisfy hunger; dress in scant saffron-colored clothing —the color of love and wisdom; must ever wander; never enter human home; must rest under trees; not sleep under one tree or on the same spot or place for three consecutive nights; never talk to or with people on any other subject than that of his search, and discuss it with humble spirit of inquiry with illumined sages he may meet on his journey.

With the first flush of the realization of Truth, he changes the color of his clothing from saffron to white, which is the color of illumination (Sattwa).

Still wandering in the ecstasy of the bliss of Truth within his soul, the objective phenomena around him seem unsubstantial.

As he roams, sporting and laughing like a boy, he becomes almost unconscious of anything outside of his soul.

To *see* him is a blessing. He has no count of time or of the phases of time—whether it is morning, noon, or night.

He feels no hunger; with the satisfaction of his *spiritual* hunger, all hunger has been satisfied forever. He is the embodiment of ecstasy, uncovered ecstasy; even his physical cover (the white cloth) has fallen from his body. He stands naked, as naked as Nature's most natural man. He is clothed with the illumination of his soul, like the Golden Age man.

. . . . . .

THE FIVE PATHS OF YOGA (Baba Bharati)

There are five paths of mental discipline by the aid of which the human soul can reach its goal quicker. These are called the five paths of Yoga, namely, Hatha, Karma, Raja, Gnana, and Bhakti.

Yoga means *union;* the same as the English word *yoke.* Yoga, therefore, in this sense, means yoking the mind to the Spirit of God by concentration.

HATHA YOGA consists in cleaning and disciplining the outer and inner physical body by the practice of certain processes of moving the muscles and fixing the eye upon some external object or the tip of the nose. These, in time, induce mental poise.

KARMA YOGA consists of performing good actions and practising spiritual formulas, which contribute to the purification of the mind and finally lead to the unfoldment of the soul.

RAJA YOGA consists of stopping the function of the mind's volitions. By volitions of the mind are meant thought-currents.

By the practice of Raja Yoga, the outflow of these thought-currents can be entirely stopped and turned inward in one concentrated stream into the soul. The main process of the shutting in of the mind-currents is by controlling the breath.

The practice of Raja Yoga has been forbidden in the Kali Yuga (Iron Age) because in this age, excepting in rare cases, the human body is too weak and delicate to stand the hardships, psychic exertions, and physical privations of its practices, and, because an adept Yogi-Guru (without whose constant help in every detail of it no student can attain the highest result) is very hard to find.

Many who now practise it under inexperienced Gurus in India meet early death, or develop incurable diseases, or even turn insane.

A moderate amount of simple breathing exercises may not be so injurious or fatal; but too much of such exercise, or the practice of the advanced rules, ought never to be attempted, especially in the West, where a proper Guru can never be found, and where people's nerves are generally shaky.

GNANA YOGA consists of an entirely mental process of Yoga, a process of discrimination between the unsubstantial and the substantial in Nature, and concentrating upon the Substantial Essence of things, and gradually getting absolutely absorbed by it.

The keeping up of this process of thought in an unbroken stream requires living a life of simplicity, solitude, and renunciation.

The life in which this thought-current becomes unbroken is the *last* life, the last incarnation of the soul. It escapes rebirth for the good for which it has worked for many incarnations.

Its separate ego is merged in the universal Ego, and finally is lost in, and becomes one with, the One-without-a-Second.

Gnana Yoga belongs to the school of the Vedanta philosophy: Vedante, fromVeda, *wisdom* and Anta, *the end*.

BHAKTI YOGA consists of concentration on the Deity through devotion, the best and highest form of Yoga; higher than all the other forms, as Krishna himself has said in the Bhagavad Gita.

Devotion is the full fruition of spiritual concentration. A true devotee is the highest Yogi.

. . . .

ANOTHER VIEW OF YOGA PHILOSOPHY

Swami Vivekananda, whose very name signifies "Bliss-in-discrimination," is well remembered on the Pacific Coast for his sensible views of the various phases of the Hindu philosophy.

In regard to the mysticism as taught by some teachers, he spoke in unmistakable terms. Of these Yoga systems he said: "Anything that is secret and mysterious in these systems of Yoga should be at once rejected. The best guide in life is strength. All mystery-mongering weakens the human brain. Through it the science of Yoga has been well-nigh destroyed.

"From the time it was discovered, more than four thousand years ago, it was perfectly delineated and formulated and preached in India; and it is a striking fact that the more modern the commentator, the greater the mistakes he makes.

"In the first place, there is no mystery in what I preach. What little I know I will tell you. So far as I can reason it out I will do so, but what I do not know I will simply tell you that is what the books say.

"A Yogi must avoid the two extremes of luxury and austerity. He must not fast, nor torture his flesh; he who does so, says the Gita, cannot be a Yogi. He who fasts, he who keeps awake, he who sleeps much, he who works too much, he who does no work; none of these can be Yogis.

"RAJA YOGA (royal yoga), the science of conquering the internal nature for the purpose of realizing the Divinity within, is divided into eight steps.

"The first is *Yama,* non-killing, non-stealing, truthfulness, continence, and non-receiving of any gifts.

"The next is *Niyama*—cleanliness, contentment, mortification, study, and self-surrender to God.

"Then came *Asana,* signifying posture; *Pranayama,* controlling the vital forces of the body; *Pratyahara,* making the mind introspective; *Dharana,* concentration; *Dhyana,* meditation; *Samedhi,* super-consciousness.

"The Yama and the Niyama, as you see, are moral trainings. Without these as a basis no practice of Yoga will succeed.

"A Yogi must not think of injuring any one through thought, word, or deed, and this applies not only to man but to all animals. Mercy shall not be for men alone, but shall go beyond and embrace the whole world."

There is surely much in the foregoing to commend itself, and yet much that is wholly beyond the nature of things to those of us who have anything to occupy mind and body in this busy workaday world. This is especially so of *Asana* (posture), of which I shall speak briefly, condensing Vivekananda's remarks as much as possible, yet obscuring nothing.

Asana (posture) is a series of exercises, physical and mental, to be gone through every day until certain higher states are reached. Therefore it is quite necessary that we should find a posture in which we can long remain.

As the main part of the action will lie along the spinal column, the one thing necessary for the posture is to hold the spinal column free, the neck, chest, and head in a straight line.

This portion of the Raja Yoga is a little similar to the Hatha Yoga, which deals entirely with the physical body, with no spiritual end in view, bodily perfection being the only aim. We have nothing to do with that here; that is in the study of Raja Yoga, because its practices are very difficult and do not lead to any spiritual growth. The result is to make men live long; health being the chief idea, the one goal of the Hatha Yoga.

The devotee is determined not to fall sick—and he never does. He lives long—a hundred years is nothing to him; he is quite young and fresh, without one hair turned gray, when he is one hundred and fifty. But that is all. A banyan-tree lives, sometimes, five thousand years; but it is a banyan-tree and nothing more. So if a man lives long, he is only a healthy animal.

The question naturally arises—Why can man not be a healthy animal and at the same time be spiritually minded? Henry Ward Beecher said, "A man with a bad liver cannot be a good Christian." To my mind, the typical healthy man is the all-around man—mentally, morally, and physically.

The Swami, after speaking as he does of the system of Hatha Yoga, especially recommends this Raja Yoga, which is quite generally known theoretically by those of us in the Western world who have followed the thought but not the practices (impracticable for us) of these sages of India.

"These exercises of Raja Yoga," says the Swami, " must be performed from three to five times at four intervals of the day; namely, before dawn, during midday, in the evening, and at midnight.

" After fifteen days to a month of practice of these exercises, stopping the right nostril with the thumb; with the left nostril draw in air, according to your capacity; then, without any interval, throw the air out through the right nostril, closing the left one. Again, inhaling through the right nostril, eject through the left, according to capacity. Then begins *Pranayama;* that is, controlling the Prana.

" The way the Hindus practise these exercises would be very difficult for this Western country. They do it from their childhood, and their lungs are prepared for it. I refer, here, more especially to Psychic Prana, which if practised irregularly may injure you."

The more you read of the Yoga exercises as practised by the Hindus and of the thoroughness of their devotion toward their ideal spiritual development, the more you will be impressed that however befitting it may be for them it is not expedient for us.

Some of the exercises have been taught in this country; some of them incorporated in some of the systems of physical training; some books have been written by a native— a native of *this* country, but with an assumed high-sounding name purporting to be that of a Yogi. These things are misleading and superficial, as they contain but a mere smattering and do not do justice to either the Yogi or his philosophy.

Take, for instance, the word *Prana,* which is frequently taught and understood to mean *breath.* Of this, Vivekananda said: "The error is the fault of the English translation. You cannot fill your being with breath but by breathing correctly you can fill it with Prana—the sum total of the cosmic energy, the vital forces of the body. Pranayama means controlling the Prana, not the breath."

"Practice is absolutely necessary," said Vivekananda. "You may sit there and listen to me by the hour every day, but if you do not practise you will never get one step further. Simply listening to explanations and theories will not do.

" There are several obstructions to practice; the first obstruction is an unhealthy body. If the body is not in a fit state, the practice will be obstructed. Therefore, to keep the body in good health, we have to take care of what we eat and drink and do, always using a mental effort."

This seems somewhat contradictory when compared with what he previously said regarding the care of the body, but he squared himself somewhat, by saying: "That is all; nothing further of the body. We must not forget that health is only a means to an end.

"When the Yogi becomes perfect there will be nothing in Nature not under his control. Yoga can be safely learned only by *direct contact* with a *teacher*."

Mark this, those of you who expect to get it from books, even those books written by the genuine teachers of India.

"If the people practise Raja Yoga, and at the same time lead an impure life, how can they expect to become Yogis?

"There must be perfect chastity in thought, word, and deed. Without it, the practice of Raja Yoga is dangerous, and may lead to insanity. The fire of Yoga burns the cage of sin that is around a man."

Beautiful thoughts are these and a beautiful life would surely result in living up to the ideal of the Hindu philosophy; but its practices, as I have said before, are impracticable, even impossible, in the Occident, however easy of attainment they may be in the Orient.

Yet, fortunately, we are not without an ideal teacher, one whose teachings can be followed by every one in every walk of life; a teacher of the purest type—the meek and lowly Nazarene.

BY A HINDU SAGE

Though fools spurn Hymen's gentle powers,
We who improve his golden hours,
By sweet experience, know
That marriage rightly understood
Gives to the tender and the good
A paradise below.

The kindest and the happiest pair
Will find concessions to forbear:
And something every day they live
To pity and, perhaps, forgive.

COMMENTS ON HINDUISM BY DR. PAUL EDWARDS

THE RESULT OF OBSERVATIONS DURING HIS EXTENSIVE TRAVELS IN INDIA

The Hindu is the most singular being alive. He will persist longer in a matter, right or wrong, than any other human being. No matter how plainly he may be shown his error, if his forefathers have done the thing, that is enough to satisfy him that his course is infallible. This stubbornness is born of ancestor-worship, the ancient and modern curse of India and China.

The Hindus manifest the utmost indifference to human life, yet show extreme solicitude for animal preservation.

When a Hindu child is born, the husband must cast away all cooking utensils. Within my own experience I knew of one husband who declined. The wife immediately committed suicide, knowing she would be despised by her neighbors when they saw no new kitchen paraphernalia. Life ceased to have any charm for her thereafter.

The tricks of the Hindus—blowing fire from the mouth, swallowing opium, the growing of the mango tree, turning a suspender into a live cobra, etc.,—must not be confounded with the exalted works of the true ascetic.

Solely of Hindu origin is what is known as the "Transmigration of Souls." The Abbe Dubois is quoted as saying, "Pythagoras learned all he knew of metempsychosis (change of soul) during his visit to India, but he never published or spoke of transmigration until his return to Greece."

Greek sages visited India during the period of 600 B. C. to A. D. 600. The philosophy of India was in its freshest bloom probably long before Abraham's time or the birth of Israel, "the chosen people of God." The great essays of Greek sages on the immortality of the soul were inspired by visits to India or Persia. In those prehistoric times all wisdom came from the East, including the great wisdom of the Egyptians.

The orthodox Brahman will never touch meat. I fully believe that the doctrine of metempsychosis alone is the cause. It is this fear of committing murder that keeps the Brahman from slaughtering animals. Metempsychosis teaches that a succession of incarnations awaits every soul; that each animal possesses a soul on its way to a human being. If, for instance, the life of an animal is taken, that soul has its progress broken and must necessarily become belated in its arrival in a human form.

The name of "East Indian" is a general term by which the inhabitants of British India are known. It is a blanket name for all the natives of India, be they Hindu, Parsi, Goanese, tricky Mohammedan, or any of the various other peoples belonging to that country. The great population is divided and subdivided into quite two hundred clans, breeds, and castes. There are over fifty-five million Mohammedans in India. They are converted Hindus; but in the conversion all the good qualities of the Hindus are lost. Numerically speaking, the Hindu is the dominant race of India. There is more of him than of all the other races combined.

PERSIAN YOGIS

Of the great Persian Yogis there have been but twenty-two; some dating back fully five thousand years B. C., others passing over into our Christian era and still influencing it. During the lives of these twenty-two Yogis nearly all the wisdom of Persia was acquired. In the seventh century A. D. Mohammed invaded Persia with a sword—which he had promised never to draw—and compelled the Persians to adopt his faith. Those who would not fled to India, where they now live about Bombay and are called Parsis. They have never recanted the Zoroastrian faith, never mixed blood with the Hindus, nor changed their style of headwear.

The Parsis, or Parsees, are the most enlightened of all the numerous races in India and the only ones benevolently inclined. The Hindu rarely opens his purse to charity, and the

Mohammedan less often. The Parsis endow benevolent institutions, maintain hospitals, and keep up their homes. They seldom become mendicants. They read foreign literature, quote the Christian Bible, and many of them are familiar with the best poets of other nations. They are frequent and persistent worshippers, and believe implicitly that Zoroaster was the greatest of saints, and that he was endowed with wisdom, religion, charity, and every other virtue over all other prophets whatsoever.

All children of the Parsis must be born on the ground floor. The mother must remain there during purification,—forty days,—when she again joins her family. When the child is five days old, a Brahman or Parsi astrologer is called. He casts the child's horoscope in hieroglyphics and then declares the exalted position to which the child will attain, and submits a long list of names for the parents' selection.

The Parsi men sup together or separately at will, but the two sexes never meet at table. This custom was derived from the Hindus.

When a son marries he brings his wife home to live; thus a single family may number scores of individuals. Until recently Parsi marriages were contracted at the age of two years for the wife and three years for the husband. It was the custom when the wives of two friends were about to become mothers, to pledge their prospective babies in wedlock, if of opposite sex. This custom has since fallen into desuetude.

The Parsi holds that sickness is the function of those who eat beyond the limits of their organs to digest. The Parsis are also fatalists. They believe that a man has a certain number of breaths allotted to him, nor can he draw another after this allotment has been exhausted.

(This is akin to our racial belief—and error—that three score and ten is the allotted span of life, and to go beyond is to live on borrowed time.)

A WONDERFUL DISCOVERY

The great traveller and world-renowned writer, Mr. Frank G. Carpenter, writing from Calcutta, May, 1910, tells of the discovery of the ashes of Buddha, which were recently found near Pashawar. They lay in a room far down under the ground below the heavy foundation of a tower which long ago was blotted from the face of the earth. The remains consist of a mass of grayish-white powder and four charred bones. Here, supposedly for about twenty-four hundred years, they have reposed undisturbed, in a crystal box inside a bronze casket. It is said there can be no doubt of the authenticity of this wonderful discovery which was made by the archæological department of the Britsh Government.

The result of this find will be to revive Buddhism, especially in India. There are between nine and ten million Buddhists in Burma, and many more in Ceylon and in parts of Farther India. Mr. Carpenter informs us that the Buddhists of Hindustan number fewer than three hundred thousand. They are found in small numbers along the northern frontier of Bengal, and upon the lower slopes of the Himalayas. In Nepal, where Buddha was born, he has yet many followers, and in Kashmir, near where his ashes were found, there are, of his believers, perhaps forty thousand all told.

The Buddha religion is the chief one of Japan; two-thirds of the Chinese are supposed to believe in it; but its most ardent followers are Thibetans and the Mongolian population of Asia.

The Buddhists are adopting the same plans of propagating their faith as are used by the Christians. They now have Buddhist Young Men's Associations corresponding to our Young Men's Christian Associations, and are now publishing tracts and distributing all sorts of religious documents.

THE BUDDHIST RELIGION

Mr. Carpenter informs us that it is a mistake to speak of the worship of Buddha. He was not looked upon as a god, but as a great teacher, a mortal man; and it was believed that any mortal might aspire to be what he was. He was regarded as the perfect man, and his life as the perfect life. Nevertheless, they pray before his shrine and use his name in their prayers.

The Buddhist religion is a belief in cause and effect. It says that man's misfortunes all come from his bad actions, and all his good from his good ones. Heaven means the extinction of his desires. This is the great end of life—to wipe out all passion, all feeling, and even all ideas. It is a sort of religious trance or ecstasy known as Nirvana. It has nothing of the worship of God; it is, in fact, practically atheistic, and is a religion of despair rather than of hope. It considers personal existence a source of evil, and that the greatest evil of mankind is birth. Were it not for that, we could not, it says, have old age, misery, and death, and we should not have to go through the long line of transmigrations by which man rises to heaven or descends to hell.

According to Buddhism, one's soul, like that of John Brown, is always marching on. The moment he dies he is born again, his soul passing at once into the form of a man, a dog, or some other animal, or worse than all, into a woman. If he escapes the latter fate he may go down, down, down through the different degrees of animal life until he falls into one of the hundred-odd Buddhist hells, which are in the middle of the earth, where the sufferers spend ten million years or more before they rise again.

The Buddhist fairy stories tell how their great teacher lived as an elephant, as a camel, as a gnat, as a swallow, or as an eagle. He went through every form of existence on the earth, in hell, and in heaven, and when he attained the perfect knowledge he could recall them all. He died a natural death in northern India at about eighty years of age.

Henry Clarke Warren says of Buddha: "He was regarded not as a mere formulator of dry metaphysical propositions, but as a very wise and compassionate friend of his fellow-man. He was full of tact, and all his ways were ways of peace. He had strong personal influence over his fellows."

Buddha denied the special virtues of caste, ritualism, and asceticism;

and insisted upon the necessity of pity, kindliness, and patience, for salvation. He taught that Nirvana is to be obtained only by escape from the causal nexus, or *Karma*, whereby the unenlightened are doomed to endless rebirths.

Buddha's "Four Truths" are: (1) Life is sorrow; (2) the chain of reincarnation results from desire; (3) the only escape is through the annihilation of desire; (4) the way of escape is the "eight-fold path" of "right belief, right resolve, right word, right act, right life, right effort, right thinking, right meditation."

We may not agree as regards the annihilation of desire, but we must acknowledge that we could not go far astray if we lived up to these eight principles. Yet the answer to the question, What *is* right belief, right resolve, etc.? would depend largely upon the individual viewpoint.

From every religious creed, and from every philosophy, we may get some good if we but look for it.